Leadership Transition

B. Vincent

Published by RWG Publishing, 2021.

LEADERSHIP TRANSITION

First edition. July 29, 2021.

Written by B. Vincent.

Also by B. Vincent

Bridge Pages
Business Acquisition
Business Bogging
Marketing Automation
Better Meetings
Conversion Optimization
Creative Solutions
Employee Recruitment
Startup Capital
Employee Mentoring
Servant Leadership
Human Resources
Team Building
Freelancing
Funnel Building
Geo Targeting
Goal Setting
Immanent List Building
Lead Generation
Leadership Course
Leadership Transition

Leadership Transition

Bruce Miller once said initiative is more similar to a mallet than a prize. You keep a prize, yet you hand off a twirly doo. Also, progression the board master Jake Appleman cautions us, senior administration groups planning for a leader change stage perhaps the most difficult obstructions in the present business world. There's no doubt. In the event that you have an authority or the board change occurring in the working environment, a lot is on the line. what you handle this will enormously mean for the eventual fate of your organization, both as far as its way of life, just as its main concern. So how would we explore the waters of such a change? How would we guarantee an adjustment of authority or the board is taken care of easily, and in a way that emphatically impacts the association for quite a long time to come? In this course, we will show you how to do precisely that.

Presidents normal residency is around three years pretty much. As indicated by a study, about 27% of leader chiefs and CEOs envisioned leftover in their situations for over five years. Differentiation this with remaining three to four years, which was at practically 32% and remaining until two years at 40%. Additionally, almost 63% of associations don't have a composed initiative progression plan. half of associations don't have a change plan by any means, refering to that they scarcely trust it to be a need.

These insights show that initiative change is an undeniably significant region that organizations should zero in on. Our course will comprise of a progression of basic conversation focuses. These are intended to cover this expansive theme as completely as conceivable to support development in these imperative regions. What's more, to work with a genuine and productive conversation inside your association about how you can each enhance this fundamental trademark both at work and in your own lives overall. A portion of these will be really protracted, and some will be moderately clear and brief. At the finish of this guide, comes the main last advance.

Conversation time, don't skirt this. This is the main piece of this preparation. At the point when you finish this course, you need to go through no less than an hour or somewhere in the vicinity going over the inquiries we supply toward the end collectively. Whoever's the big cheese on the gathering should assign a facilitator whose duty it is that each question is covered, and that everybody time allowing, can express their opinion, ensure all commitments are esteemed, all ideas considered, and all sentiments regarded. So how about we move into the main conversation point. Get your work done. What got you in the position may not be sufficient afterward. So don't take enormous actions presently. All things considered, evaluate what your position expects of you. At the point when you are missing, or don't have a sufficiently high expertise level of you've then, at that point had the opportunity to cure those regions. Consider everything about the organization. To make it simpler for you. It's ideal to make a guide of how force functions in your association, and among your partners. Remember to watch out for your association's way of life as well.

As a CEO, you must realize how everything works. So here are the five fundamental elements of administration, which are as per the following the business' techniques and activities the association's corporate culture the staff The actual pioneers and your different partners. When assessing your association, you don't have to go far for data. You've effectively got the best sources readily available, like the past CEO, your staff, just as retailers or providers, and your clients. lay the basis for the basic jobs in your organization. upper administration ought to think about every single basic job inside the organization. There ought to be reinforcement plans for all jobs in the event of opening. Guarantee there's an advancement plan and progression plan for each position. When you have plans for moving new individuals into senior level positions, return to them depending on the situation, and consistently. Recollect that you ought to return to your arrangements for your CEO the most one your organization required only a couple a long time earlier may not be the most ideal decision from now into the foreseeable future. Your present decision of CEO might require some additional guidance to appropriately lead the association. So ensure your arrangements fit your current circumstance perfectly. Five significant stages. authority change has five phases which are crisis progression arranging. Here the board readies a rundown of potential individuals who can assume control over the duties depending on the situation. progress arranging, where the pioneer designs their own takeoff from the association progression arranging. This sees the association making arrangements for the takeoff of the current chief initiative change, where the upper administration declares the CEOs moving toward flight. Be that as it may, generally they deal with the inside and outside connections and determination of another pioneer, Interim or something else. Crisis progression arranging the directorate ought to have crisis designs set up before they begin looking for a more drawn out term pioneer. Their main concern shouldn't track down a between time CEO. They shouldn't simply call it done in the wake of picking one individual. The board needs to have a rundown of expected possibility to browse. Consider it having a reinforcement chief in the event that the CEO becomes excessively ill to appropriately carry out their responsibilities or needs to deal with some family matters, or are being held back from serving the organization because of catastrophic events. The board can work together with HR in regards to the rundown.

Here are the rudiments of making an overall crisis plan. Record key data, for example, passwords and ledger subtleties. Additionally observe protection approaches, financing responsibilities, allows at present in measure associations with contacts, and your providers and merchants. Furthermore, you need to make a rundown of crisis contacts for every one of your representatives. Set up off site reinforcement as well as cloud based capacity. That is on the off chance that you don't as of now have either. Along these lines, there's no possibility of losing the organization's relevant records and data.

Set up your crisis progression plans characterize who's in control on the off chance that one individual in a general position can't satisfy their obligations. It's basic that your hierarchy of leadership doesn't break. So you must have reinforcement possibility for your reinforcement competitors. The Transition Plan whether the timings more broad, or more explicit, the active CEOs takeoff date should be set up. This will take into consideration the organization to have adequate opportunity to plan for the afternoon. These are the inquiries to pose your destined to withdraw CEO as you make a change plan. When will you leave the organization? After your flight? Will you be resigning by and large? Or on the other hand will you fill in as an advisor? Will you be an advisor for this organization or for another? Are there any particularly huge activities that you'd prefer to complete before your takeoff? Observe chances are these will not complete by them. What do you figure the approaching chief would profit with what openings do you think could help them what ought to be their needs? What ought to be done to help or support the board or Executive Committee while the progress interaction is continuous, and what ought to be done to help and build up the authority group? The progression plan. This relies chiefly upon the association's response to the pioneers takeoff, especially with the course of events and cycle. The actual response contrasts from one organization to another. Yet, here are instances of potential activities the governing body can take when a progress occurs. Elevate inward staff to the position have an interval chief quest for another pioneer converge with another association, spin off projects or stop tasks. activity steps whatever move your association will make the cycles following that are as yet unchanged. One set the CEOs progress date in stone to meet with the board seat and its chief individuals to talk about the future condition of subsidizing, staffing, just as the organization's projects. The chances and obstacles for the association as introduced by the change.

The combining merging or ending of projects, who will principally deal with the progress interaction, maybe the chief advisory group or a totally new board. Three, talk with the whole board or the leader council to examine all that you talked about in the past advance. So obviously, the future condition of subsidizing, staffing, just as the organization's projects, the chances and obstacles for the association as introduced by the change, the blending, combining or ending of projects, and who will basically deal with the progress interaction for pinpoint the assets required for the enlistment cycle. This includes subsidizing time and labor. Five, get ready to inside and remotely declared the current chiefs flight by making an underlying correspondence plan. It's principally intended to come from the board, however the leaving chiefs info would be exceptionally esteemed. Six, ask yourself, what do you have to occur for board enrollment and preparing all through the cycle? Seven. Likewise, do you require extra essential arranging work done? This is to help the choice and afterward the onboarding of your picked new pioneer. Hello ate secretly address the leaders to start the employing cycle. Also, nine, the active CEO should refresh three things. The crisis plan, the strategy, and the advancement plan. Best to have previous duplicates to make your work simpler. Keys to Success and progression to guarantee a smooth and fruitful progression measure. Here are five keys to progress.

The Board of Directors must be educated about administration progression and how best to go about it. They should commit time and exertion to picking a fine chief and afterward assist with establishing an inviting climate for said pioneer whenever they've been introduced. A supervisory group ought to be set up to help the progress along this group should be given satisfactory opportunity to deal with the change interaction, particularly since it's notwithstanding their all around present undertakings. Should the association not have a supervisory group. The board should designate extra staff or even re-appropriate volunteers to accomplish the work. There ought to be a forward-thinking key strategy that epitomizes the association's objectives, vision and mission. This will reflect and bring about discovering a pioneer who can additionally profit the organization's future. Assets should likewise be assigned for the progression interaction. This remembers contributing for the staff and the directorate. Try not to take a gander at the progression interaction as a misfortune for the organization. Consider it rather as a chance for everybody required for the leaving chief, the association partners, and obviously, the actual association. Advance demonstrated and proficient workers. While contemplating a replacement for your leaving chief, you'll need to keep your entryways open for your present staff who are qualified for the position, they need to have a battling opportunity to substantiate themselves to you. This will dispense with the inclination that you're playing top choices, or that you don't have confidence in their capacities. In case there's truly somebody in the organization who's similarly pretty much as refined and experienced as the newbie you're thinking about, why not pick the previous.

The benefit is that an inside up-and-comers previously found out about how the organization functions, so they don't should be raised to speed on that record. Nonetheless, your competitor must be viewed as a capable, achieved pioneer to be acknowledged by their companions. Something else, those friends will loathe them. You may likewise apply profession way change key execution pointers, which are essentially evaluating frameworks that can be useful while picking the best possibility for the situation of CEO. When the outcomes are free, an unbiased board of judges audits them, guaranteeing a fair-minded choice to the workers. A difference in authority acquires a component of vulnerability. Furthermore, you as a worker may be uncomfortable with what occurs straightaway, keep a watch out what your new chief brings to the table while tactfully surveying them. As you do that, ensure you don't fall behind on your undertakings. Whenever you've found out about who your manager is, you would then be able to have a more significant discussion with them. It's presumably somewhat forward, yet one of you needs to make the initial step, you can get the discussion going by telling them your objectives throughout everyday life, especially those disturbing the organization. You can likewise share some non organization related objectives, which will assist with making all the difference for the discussion and decrease both your uneasiness. Furthermore, there's another method to submit yourself as a determined worker is to ask your new manager straightforwardly for their assessment on your exhibition whenever. Regardless of whether it's not time for execution audits. You must adjust to change and do what must be finished. stay on top of things in any capacity you can. Your commitments to the organization enormous or little, will help your manager hugely. To keep up with entomb group connections. Advancing somebody can get somewhat precarious as you the upper administration need to ensure it's not something that just emerged from the blue. A few group will feel sore that they weren't considered for the situation, obviously, is upper administration picking the ideal individual for the work is inside your circumspection. Be that as it may, in doing as such, you should try not to cause blocage to trust and the organization. Openly clarify why you picked a specific individual for the work. Else, it will cause a crack between the approaching CEO and an unforeseen of the organization who feel they are a superior decision or don't really accept that that your decision ought to be in such a position. once again introduce the new pioneer to everybody. As you do this, you'll reference the prior connections. However, you additionally put down new stopping points and make the now CEOs authority exceptionally understood. This is what to do. Tell the staff unmistakably the reasons why you decided to advance them. unmistakably clarify additionally how the change will continue. Clarify why you're invigorated for your decision. Assist your staff with understanding that the connection among them and the approaching CEO will be diverse pushing ahead. Request that the group support the new supervisor. In like manner, support the group by checking in at standard stretches to perceive how they network with their new chief.

During the progress, develop the new supervisor by giving them the instruments to lead well train them on a case by case basis. Support yourself for some hard real factors. You will understand that you will be powerless in the year that it takes for your CEO to truly adjust, you must be ready for the easing back down of the easing back down of raising money energy, the board limit and aptitude to either debilitate or be lost funder connections to either debilitate or be lost by and large. key partners and vital associations to be waiting or debilitate or be lost by and large. The deficiency of key information, the abdication of staff a critical payout for your active chiefs accumulated get-away time, the increment of your approaching CEO compensation to reflect current market rate load up individuals to leave the general culture of the organization to change the new CEO to not be able to advocate the organization's objectives and missions for some time. Also, the top managerial staff to encounter burnout just as feel withdrew from the progress. Have faith in your representatives as the administration, you must urge your workers to take risks and decide. This will engage them to give them a feeling of certainty. Your workers would then be able to proceed to turn out to be new pioneers, putting your association on the way to significance. Cultivate pioneers effectively present in your organization, prepared them to one day assume control for future opportunities. You must furnish your representatives with administration preparing and openings. This isn't just for them to test their guts, but on the other hand it will get individuals around them to see them as pioneers by their own doing. This will help their picture whenever you've chosen to make them your contender for more significant level positions. You could be perched on the following CEO. All you need are the right preparing and change plans. An interior applicant is worthwhile on the grounds that said competitor definitely knows the manners in which things are done around the association. Also more youthful pioneers are more anxious to secure information and to participate in preparing. Accomplice them up with tutors who can help and further their development. The board needs to chip away at making arrangements for crisis progressions, getting ready for long haul progressions, monetary ventures, ability dealing with, especially the capability of your expected applicants, and you will hazard appraisal meetings just as the executives conversations. Try not to pass on your CEO to their own gadgets after they've been introduced. In the event that you have an extraordinary onboarding plan set up, your new CEO will not experience any difficulty adjusting to their new job. That, yet you need to consistently uphold them, and not simply pass on them to deal with their own. Examination has demonstrated that fruitful onboarding can viably set up your new CEO for what's to come. You'll likewise see some different advantages, like reducing the opportunity of CEO turnover, laying out the groundwork for the organization later on. You will reinforce the connection between the CEO and the Board of Directors and permitting the CEO to share and adjust their essential vision. So the arrangement expects you to set up execution goals. Get your needs straight. These are chiefly inside a timeframe that traverses only a couple months, think 30 days, 60 days, 90 days. Next up are the more extended term objectives. These are to be done inside the two or three months a short time later. For instance, a half year or a year or year and a half. obviously characterize what you expect of the governing body, the CEO and the staff. Give your chief some preparation. This additionally enjoys an optional benefit as the board and others taking care of the preparation will actually want to assemble a bond with them. Make and have frameworks of assessment to quantify progress. Get funders engaged with the onboarding program, especially with contributing. Remember about your leaving CEO. You need a procedure to off board your active CEO while making an arrangement for them. Put down rules and stopping points and be clear. Above all else, don't feel abnormal conversing with your leaving CEO about off loading up, they will wouldn't fret that much. they've actually got a job to carry out as well. So don't simply release them and never converse with them again. It's not important to put them on the top managerial staff at this time all things considered. However, do take note of that the leaving CEO actually takes part in contributor and funder connections. They've been supporting the organization for quite a long time, and have left an imprint on the association that can't be downplayed.

The board should manage how the active chief will spend their last days as CEO. how they'll be honored, can help the new CEO, and what their job will be whenever they've changed. The board and authority groups should cooperate so that all records and cycles and so forth, are easily carried out too. To the withdrawing pioneers, don't allow feelings to take control. This is an interaction of progression. Rather than an interaction of substitution. It's normal for it to occur. Relax, the organization will not discard you, you can in any case have a major effect. In case you're struggling acclimating to the change, you can request that somebody help you out, like a mentor. How to get the hard conversations rolling? Here are a few inquiries the board seat can use to lead into progression talks. What will the organization resemble after our present CEO has left? Is it accurate to say that we are the board prepared to get a change cycle in progress? When and how would we expect that a progress is going to occur? How would we begin wanting to progress? Is there a requirement for an interval time we look for a lasting CEO? Do we know the association's bearing? Well? Do we have a sufficient feeling of it for the following modest bunch of years? Presently here are a few inquiries the CEO can use to lead into progression talk. What will my life resemble? After I've left my post? How does the organization look now? In what state will I leave it in? Does the board require some help dealing with the change? Does the staff require some help taking care of the progress?

How would I prepare my staff for the change? The onboarding. Try not to stop with the progress cycle the second your new forerunners set up, guide the new pioneer with plans and instructing. Since the accomplishment of your chief will be resolved in the initial not many months of their residency. Everybody should cooperate to help the CEO. HR has a considerable amount to do as of now. So the governing body should endeavor to guarantee the CEOs smooth onboarding.

The whole association ought to offer their help, and a coach or mate can take care of your CEO. Particularly whenever said tutor feels comfortable around the organization and the requirements of the situation to the pioneers. recognize that you don't have the foggiest idea what you don't have a clue. You'll need to speak with the board frequently and have an arrangement that works with what the board needs. So you can both push ahead in amicability. serve your representatives. You must express your objectives proactively to fill in as an illustration to your staff. Your Goals should be practical and feasible. What's more, in particular, you must have the option to focus on them. You'll acquire regard among your workers by taking care of business. So follow through on your guarantees and satisfying arrangements. Here several different things that will tell your representatives that you're here to serve them. arrive as expected for gatherings with your new staff. Come to work with an uplifting outlook that will come off on everybody. Welcome them toward the beginning of the day. Pose them basic inquiries on how they're doing that day. say thanks to them for their commitments, supplement their qualities.

Praise the organization's victories as regularly as could really be expected. Authority advances are unimaginably significant.

Significant Level advances are vital. They'll affect the business in a manner that can't be disregarded. If that is to benefit the organization, will rely upon the activities your new chief will take. On the off chance that the change is achievement, As indeed, incredible things will occur for the organization. Yet, in the event that the change isn't fruitful, you can say farewell to those helps. Put down your stopping points with tasks and stop doings. Set up a quit doing list close by a daily agenda for the organization, you'll must be unequivocal and thin down all that you're wanting to do, and not do. The term of these rundowns can last maybe for various months, or possibly until the finish of your residency. It's incredible to have these rundowns as they'll keep you and your endeavors centered. Else, you or your staff may grow more than needed. A benevolent group of workers may require on a specific exertion that you hadn't prevented them from. What's more, it probably won't work out well, costing the organization significant assets that might have been utilized to fuel the drives that you needed to occur. Discover things you can add to your rundown at the earliest opportunity. What would you be able to postpone or hold, or put in into things like drives, measures, exercises, reports, and so on Be as explicit as possible. Backing your chief.

Individuals commit errors no doubt, individuals commit a ton of errors when they're managing something new or new to them. It would be valuable for the CEO to have somebody go about as their aide. This somebody can turn into an emotionally supportive network for the CEO. They'll turn into an associate and a sounding board for thoughts, you can welcome on an administrator or specialist who knows about the CEO job. Be that as it may, you can likewise set up the approaching CEO by having them beforehand be the CEO. This will help the approaching chief realize beyond any doubt what to do in their future situation as they've straightforwardly noticed the CEO. Also, we'll have the option to proceed with the CEOs work flawlessly. This way both the CEO and the board can both assess the future chiefs progress and afterward give criticism as fundamental. On the off chance that time doesn't take into account the approaching chief to work with the active chief, then, at that point they ought to basically go through one on one preparing time. It's significant for the current CEO to grant their insight to set up the CEO with critical data while they're actually present, and working at the organization. Also, presently, it's conversation time. The main piece of this preparation whoever's the big enchilada in the gathering should assign a facilitator whose obligation it is that every one of the inquiries you see on your screen is covered and that everybody time allowing, can express their opinion, ensure all commitments are esteemed. All ideas considered and all conclusions regarded.

Don't miss out!

Visit the website below and you can sign up to receive emails whenever B. Vincent publishes a new book. There's no charge and no obligation.

https://books2read.com/r/B-A-QWUO-RHVQB

BOOKS 2 READ

Connecting independent readers to independent writers.

Also by B. Vincent

Affiliate Marketing
Affiliate Marketing
Affiliate Marketing

Standalone
Affiliate Recruiting
Business Layoffs & Firings
Business and Entrepreneur Guide
Business Remote Workforce
Career Transition
Project Management
Precision Targeting
Professional Development
Strategic Planning
Content Marketing
Imminent List Building
Getting Past GateKeepers
Banner Ads
Bookkeeping

Bridge Pages
Business Acquisition
Business Bogging
Marketing Automation
Better Meetings
Conversion Optimization
Creative Solutions
Employee Recruitment
Startup Capital
Employee Mentoring
Servant Leadership
Human Resources
Team Building
Freelancing
Funnel Building
Geo Targeting
Goal Setting
Immanent List Building
Lead Generation
Leadership Course
Leadership Transition

About the Publisher

Accepting manuscripts in the most categories. We love to help people get their words available to the world.

Revival Waves of Glory focus is to provide more options to be published. We do traditional paperbacks, hardcovers, audio books and ebooks all over the world. A traditional royalty-based publisher that offers self-publishing options, Revival Waves provides a very author friendly and transparent publishing process, with President Bill Vincent involved in the full process of your book. Send us your manuscript and we will contact you as soon as possible.

Contact: Bill Vincent at rwgpublishing@yahoo.com www.rwgpublishing.com

www.ingramcontent.com/pod-product-compliance
Lightning Source LLC
Chambersburg PA
CBHW030537210326
41597CB00014B/1181